I0440807

Pandas

Fun Facts and Cool Pictures of these Adorable Creatures

By Laura Han

Copyright © 2014 Laura Han

All rights reserved.

ISBN-13: 978-1502549181

ISBN-10: 1502549182

Table of Contents

Author's Statement

All Rights Reserved. No part of this publication may be reproduced, used in any form or by any electronic or mechanical means including information storage and retrieval systems without the written permission from the author except in the case of a reviewer who may quote brief passages in a review.

Dedication

This book is dedicated to children all round the world who love Pandas and are inquisitive about the environment they live in.

Let's show we care by making efforts, however small, to save these wonderful animals from disappearing from our planet so we can enjoy them for many generations to come!

Laura Han

The Magical Giant Panda

Have you ever been to the zoo or seen the wonderful pictures of pandas and wonder how they live? Giant Pandas have been around for thousands of years and are one of the rarest mammals in the world. In olden times, the Emperor used to keep pandas as pets in their gardens. They were considered very precious and were dearly admired by all. Many scholars also believed Pandas were like a semi-divine animal that had magical powers able to fight off natural disasters and bad spirits. The giant panda was totally unknown outside the secretive "Middle Kingdom" until towards the end of the 19th century.

Pandas live high up in the mountains among thick forests in China, where there is a lot of rain and mist throughout the year as well as thick snow in the winter. Pandas love their environment as long as there is plenty of bamboo growing and open space to wander about. They are good tree climbers too as they can easily reach to the top of trees and sleep between the branches.

How Big Is A Panda?

If you have never seen a Giant Panda in person, then you might have to use your imagination as they are much bigger than you think. When Giant Pandas are fully grown, the males can weigh as much as 300 pounds (140 kgs) and stand as tall as five feet (1.5 meters). The males are much larger than the females, but many of the females still get to over 200 pounds (90 kgs). Their name means large bear-cat.

Scientists have debated for a long time whether the giant panda belongs to the bear family or to the raccoon family. But now they are sure the panda is a bear and its distantly related cousin the red panda is more of a raccoon. Red pandas are a much smaller animal, a little larger than a house-cat. They feed on bamboo but also eat fruits, plants and insects. Red pandas are nocturnal animals that are found in the forests of Nepal, Burma and China.

Panda's Special Coat

Panda bears are famous for their unique black and white appearance. They look like other bears in their shape but have very distinctive markings. All giant pandas have black patches around their eyes and black ears on a white head. Their legs are black and there is a black band across their backs. Their mid sections are pinkish white. Some think this color works to help the bears to hide in the snow and rocks. Giant panda fur is coarse, dense and somewhat oily. Their thick fur acts like a coat to keep them warm and dry in the chilly mountain forests. Pandas do not store much fat in their bodies so they do not hibernate during the winter months. Instead they will seek shelter in hollow trees.

Where Do Pandas Live?

Giant Pandas once roamed freely over a large part of Asia. Today, their home is only limited to six mountain ranges in Southwestern China. Over the last 30 years, Sichuan Province where Pandas come from has lost nearly one third of its forests and other vegetation. The expansion of homes and farms has made life very difficult for pandas to survive in the wild.

Pandas have to move higher up in the mountains just to stay safe and find enough food to live. Their habitat is now in protected Nature Reserves which are half zoo and half park, where there are special facilities to care for Pandas and help them to breed. There are 40 Giant Panda reserves in China. These reserves need to be connected via corridors in order to reduce the isolation and splitting-up of the Giant Panda population.

What Do Pandas Feast On?

Pandas love their bamboo – which makes up the biggest part of their diet – nearly 95%. That is like eating the same thing every day for 9 meals! Their favorite parts are the stalks, shoots and leaves.

Bamboo is a plant that grows quickly in thick forests. Pandas are well known for their huge appetite for this treat. They will often eat for 14 hours in one day! And they can eat anywhere from 25 pounds (11 kgs) to 40 pounds (18 kgs) of bamboo each day. That is a lot more food than we humans can eat!

Giant Pandas have a special bone in their paws. They use this bone in the same way humans use their thumbs for gripping food. They are able to hold the bamboo and bite into the stalks. Pandas are most often seen eating in a seated position. They put their hind legs in front and sit almost like a person. Sometimes, they also like to snack lying on their backs. As these bears spend a lot of time munching, they seem to have found the best way to do it!

Bamboo grows well in China and Panda Bears can eat mainly four different kinds of bamboo. Pandas hate bamboo rats which are often found burrowed underground and they would eat them up quickly before the roots get ruined by the rats.

Pandas that live in zoos don't get the same diet. They do eat bamboo but also get sugar cane, rice gruel, apples, carrots and sweet potatoes. Pandas do get a lot of water from the bamboo stalks, but it isn't quite enough for their large bodies. So, they will drink water from streams and lakes to keep them from being thirsty.

How Long Is A Panda's Lifespan?

In the wild, pandas will live to about 25-30 years old. Those in zoos live longer. The longest living panda was Mei Mei who lived in a Chinese zoo until the age of 36. Pandas spend quite a bit of time growing up.

Female Pandas don't have babies until they are about 4 to 8 years old. They have a very short time to find a male partner every year. So, this makes it harder to keep the panda population growing. Most of the time a mamma will have one baby. If she ever has two, the weaker one will die. Pandas can have babies until they are about 20 years old.

Baby Pandas

Even though the Giant Panda weighs up to 300 pounds (140 kgs), the baby panda is weeny tiny! Weighing only about 5 ounces (140 grams), it is only the size of a stick of butter! The newborn babies called cubs are born pink, hairless and blind. The baby panda is the smallest newborn compared to the size of the parent. It works out that it would take 900 baby pandas to make the size of one grown up panda - that is heaps of growing!

The panda mother is very caring; she will hold the cub close to her chest for weeks and covers it with her large paws. This is to protect the cub from predators like the snow leopard and the giant eagle that will eat baby pandas.

Little cubs don't move around until they are almost 3 months old. By the time they are one year old, the cubs can survive on bits of bamboo but they will stay with their mothers for two years before leaving on their own.

What Do Pandas Do All Day?

Pandas are slow movers! They almost seem clumsy when they walk. Adult Pandas spend most of their time wandering and looking for food. Remember how much they eat? They also relax and rest often.

Younger pandas, however, are friendly and very playful. They run and chase each other, climb trees and tumble all over the ground. Giant Pandas are truly "roly poly" creatures when they play.

Pandas are actually quite talkative compared to other bears. They roar when angry, snort, growl, bleat and honk to let other bears know to stay away! Even though they like to make noise, they are rather shy and not very social with other pandas. They seem happy being on their own in their leisurely lifestyle.

What Can We Do To Save The Pandas?

Scientist estimate there are only 1,600 pandas left in the wild and about another 300 living in zoos across the world. Much help is needed to save the pandas from disappearing. Apart from the loss of their natural habitat due dramatic increases in human settlement, pandas must also deal with natural disasters.

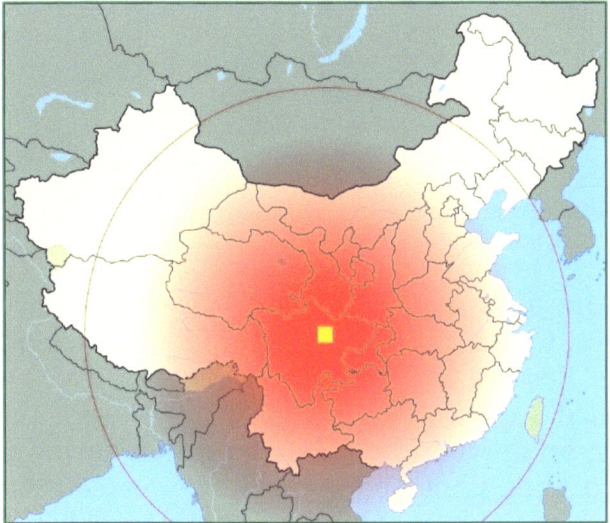

In May 12th 2008, the powerful earthquake in Sichuan Province, China happened just a few miles from the Wolong Nature Reserve Center where pandas lived. Aftershocks continued for days and many pandas were injured, went missing or starved to death. The quake buried much of the bamboo trees under tons and tons of rock and mud. As a result, the government had to act very quickly to relocate the pandas to a safe place.

We can all help these beautiful bears to survive by finding out about Wildlife Reserves in your neighborhood using the internet or at the library. Good zoos provide facts about their animals and may be carrying out conservation breeding programs. Ask if they need volunteers or you could contact an international conservation organization and join in their efforts to preserve the bamboo forests from further destruction, so that pandas can continue to live and grow. We must save bamboo seeds too and sending them to the right places will help in some way.

Teaching our friends about Pandas and joining Support groups can bring more attention to save this rare, endangered animal. This way, we can enjoy them when we become grown-ups and have kids of our own!

Thank You

Dear Readers

Thank you for reading my Book. I hope you have enjoyed learning about Pandas and the special environment they live in. Please leave your comments and provide a review of my book at http://tinyurl.com/njwmhnc – I would be most appreciative.

Best wishes,

Laura Han

www.ingramcontent.com/pod-product-compliance
Lightning Source LLC
Chambersburg PA
CBHW050924290526
45792CB00002B/881